YOKOHAMA

VACATION GUIDE

2023

The Essential and Ultimate Guide to Yokohama's Hotels, Cuisines, Shopping Tips, Insider's Tips, Top Attractions, History, and Culture

ALFRED FLORES

Copyright © 2023, Alfred Flores

TABLE OF CONTENTS

INTRODUCTION

CHAPTER ONE:

Getting to Know Yokohama

   Geographical Overview

   Climate and Weather

   History and Culture

   Festivals and Events

CHAPTER TWO:

Planning Your Trip to Yokohama

   Best Time to Visit

   Visa and Travel Requirements

   How to Get There

   Getting Around

   Accommodations Options

   Travel Insurance

CHAPTER THREE:

Yokohama's Top Attractions

Yokohama Chinatown

Minato Mirai 21

Sankeien Garden

Yamashita Park

Landmark Tower and Sky Garden

CHAPTER FOUR:

Yokohama's Cultural Heritage

Yokohama Museum of Art

Yokohama Red Brick Warehouse

Yokohama Port Museum

Yokohama Noh Theater

Yokohama Silk Museum

CHAPTER FIVE:

Exploring Yokohama's Neighborhoods

Kannai and Noge

Motomachi and Yamate

Yokohama Bay Area

Yokohama Station Area

Key Highlights in Yokohama Station Area:

Yokohama Stadium and Chinatown

CHAPTER SIX:
Yokohama's Culinary Scene
  Traditional Japanese Cuisine
  Yokohama Ramen
  Seafood and Sushi
  Izakayas and Yakitori
  Yokohama Craft Beer and Sake

CHAPTER SEVEN:
Hidden Gems in Yokohama
  Yamate Italian Garden
  Orbi Yokohama
  Shomyo-ji Temple
  Yokohama Curry Museum
  Nogeyama Zoo

CHAPTER EIGHT:
Outdoor Activities in Yokohama
  Yamashita Park and Seaside Promenade

Jogashima Island

Hakkeijima Sea Paradise

Mitsuike Park

Yokohama Cosmo World

CHAPTER NINE:

Shopping and Souvenirs in Yokohama

Yokohama World Porters

Yokohama Landmark Plaza

Yokohama AkaRenga Soko

Yokohama Bay Quarter

Yokohama Motomachi Shopping Street

CHAPTER TEN:

Nightlife and Entertainment in Yokohama

Bars and Clubs in Kannai

Jazz Bars in Noge

Yokohama Symphony Orchestra

Music Venues Live

Yokohama Cinema Scene

CHAPTER ELEVEN:

Yokohama's Maritime History

  Yokohama Port Opening Memorial Hall

  NYK Maritime Museum

  Kanagawa Prefectural Museum of Cultural History

  Nippon Maru and Yokohama Osanbashi Pier

CHAPTER TWELVE:

Practical Information for Travelers

  Transportation Options

  Money and Currency Exchange

  Language and Cultural Etiquette

  Safety Tips and Emergency Contacts

  Health and Medical Services

CHAPTER THIRTEEN:

Appendix

  30 Useful Phrases in Japanese with Pronunciation Guide

  Currency Conversion Chart

Packing List for Yokohama

Hand-Picked Hotel Recommendations for Every Budget

MAP OF YOKOHAMA

INTRODUCTION

Welcome to Yokohama! This guide is designed to introduce you to the beautiful city of Yokohama, Japan, and provide you with essential information to make the most of your visit. Whether you're a first-time traveler or a seasoned explorer, Yokohama has something to offer for everyone.

Welcome to Yokohama

Yokohama is a vibrant and dynamic city located in the Kanagawa Prefecture, just south of Tokyo, Japan. With a population of over three million people, it is Japan's second-largest city and serves as an integral part of the Greater Tokyo Area. The city is nestled between the Tokyo Bay and the rugged hills, making for a stunning contrast of natural landscapes and urban development.

Steeped in history and culture, Yokohama has transformed from a small fishing village in the mid-19th century to a bustling port city and an international metropolis. Its international influences are evident in its architecture, cuisine, and diverse communities that welcome people from all around the world.

Why Visit Yokohama?

Yokohama is a city of unique charm and offers a plethora of attractions and experiences that cater to different interests:

- Scenic Landscapes: From the iconic Yokohama Bay area with its stunning waterfront views to the beautiful parks and gardens scattered throughout the city, Yokohama boasts breathtaking natural landscapes that provide a refreshing escape from urban life.

- Cultural Treasures: Delve into Yokohama's history and cultural heritage by exploring its numerous museums, galleries, and historic buildings. The city's rich past can be seen in places like Sankeien Garden, Yokohama Red Brick Warehouse, and the Yokohama Museum of Art.

- Cosmopolitan Vibes: Yokohama's diverse population has resulted in a vibrant mix of cultures and a wide array of international restaurants, bars, and shops. The city's cosmopolitan ambiance makes it an exciting place to experience global influences.

- Shopping and Entertainment: From upscale shopping malls to quirky boutiques, Yokohama offers an excellent shopping experience for fashion enthusiasts and souvenir hunters alike. Additionally, the city is known for its lively entertainment scene, including theaters, music venues, and nightclubs.

- Cuisine: Food lovers will be delighted by the diverse culinary scene in Yokohama. From fresh seafood delicacies to traditional Japanese dishes and international cuisines, the city has something to satisfy every palate.

How to Use This Guide

This guide is designed to be your companion during your visit to Yokohama. It is organized into different sections, each focusing on different aspects of the city. Here's how you can use this guide effectively:

- Sightseeing: Discover the must-visit attractions and landmarks in Yokohama, along with tips on how to get there and the best times to visit.

- Activities: Find exciting things to do in Yokohama, including cultural experiences, outdoor adventures, and family-friendly activities.

- Dining: Explore the diverse culinary scene in Yokohama, with recommendations for popular restaurants, local delicacies, and food streets.

- Shopping: Learn about the best shopping spots in the city, from traditional markets to modern shopping complexes.

- Accommodation: Get information on different types of accommodations available in Yokohama, from luxury hotels to budget-friendly hostels.

- Transportation: Understand the transportation options in Yokohama, including how to navigate the city using public transport.

- Safety and Etiquette: Familiarize yourself with essential safety tips and cultural etiquette to ensure a respectful and pleasant stay.

Yokohama: Quick Facts and Statistics

- **Population:** Over three million residents (as of 2021).

- **Area:** Approximately 437 square kilometers.

- **Language:** Japanese is the official language, but English is widely spoken in tourist areas.

- **Currency:** Japanese Yen (JPY).

- **Climate:** Yokohama experiences a humid subtropical climate with hot summers and mild winters.

- **Landmarks:** Yokohama Landmark Tower, Yokohama Chinatown, Yamashita Park, and the Cup Noodles Museum are among the city's famous landmarks.

Now that you have a brief overview of Yokohama, you're ready to embark on a journey of exploration and discovery in this captivating city. Enjoy your stay and make the most of your time in Yokohama!

CHAPTER ONE:
Getting to Know Yokohama

Yokohama, a city with a rich history and dynamic culture, offers an intriguing fusion of tradition and contemporary. This chapter will examine the geography, the weather, the enthralling history, and the exciting festivals and events that make Yokohama such a memorable place to visit.

Geographical Overview

Yokohama is situated in the Kanagawa Prefecture on the eastern coast of Japan's main island, Honshu. It is conveniently located just south of Tokyo and is a part of the Greater Tokyo Area, making it simple to get to from the nation's capital. The Tanzawa Mountains to the west, the Miura Peninsula to the south, and Tokyo Bay to the east all encircle the city.

Yokohama's geographical diversity is a defining feature of its landscape. The picturesque waterfront along the Tokyo Bay is an iconic area where visitors can enjoy stunning views of the ocean and take leisurely strolls along the promenades. The city is also blessed with numerous parks and gardens, providing green spaces and a welcome respite from the urban hustle.

Climate and Weather

A humid subtropical climate prevails in Yokohama, with hot, muggy summers and comparatively moderate winters. Here is a breakdown of the weather by season:

- Spring (March to May): The season of spring offers Yokohama moderate temperatures and cherry blossoms. This is among the greatest seasons to go since the parks and gardens of the city spring to life with stunning cherry blossoms, providing an amazing sight.

- Summer (June to August): Yokohama's summers can be hot and muggy, with frequent highs of 30°C (86°F). During this time, visitors should use sun protection and stay hydrated since there may be some light rains.

- Autumn (September to November): Autumn brings Yokohama comfortable weather and colorful greenery. This is yet another wonderful time of year for touring as the city's parks and gardens take on vivid shades of red, orange, and yellow.

- Winter (December to February): Yokohama's winters are typically pleasant, with a few days below freezing. Even though snowfall in the city is uncommon, it can still be cool and rainy, so visitors should consider layering up.

History and Culture

Beginning in the early 17th century, Yokohama was a modest fishing village. However, it rose to prominence in the middle of the 19th century when Japan, after years of isolation, opened its ports to foreign trade. Yokohama quickly developed into a thriving port city and a hub for trade and business worldwide.

Foreign cultures have had a significant impact on the history of the city, particularly during the Meiji era. The Yokohama Port's construction allowed for the influx of numerous foreign communities, including British, Chinese, American, and others. The cosmopolitan atmosphere that resulted from this exposure to the outside world still exists today.

Yokohama is home to a variety of museums, art galleries, and cultural organizations that honor the city's history and modern expressions. The Yokohama Museum of Art, which houses a varied collection of Japanese and Western art, is open to visitors. Those who want to learn more about the history of the city can visit the Yokohama History Museum.

Festivals and Events

The city of Yokohama often hosts festivals and events that give visitors an opportunity to get a feel for the city's vibrant culture and sense of community. Some notable festivals and events include:

- Yokohama Chinatown Spring Festival: This vibrant celebration of Chinese New Year features jovial parades, age-old entertainment, and delectable Chinese food.

- Yokohama Port Festival: This May celebration honors the debut of Yokohama Port and includes a dazzling fireworks show over the water, a spectacular parade, and musical performances.

- Yokohama Jazz Promenade: Jazz fans will adore this yearly event in October, when jazz music performances take place at a variety of Yokohama venues.

- Yokohama Red Brick Warehouse Oktoberfest: Modeled after the well-known German celebration, this autumnal gathering offers a taste of German food, beer, and live music in a festive setting.

- Yokohama International Film Festival: The Yokohama International Film Festival, which features a wide variety of foreign and Japanese films and draws filmmakers and moviegoers from all over the world, is a treat for moviegoers.

These celebrations and activities are only a few instances of how Yokohama celebrates its rich cultural past and offers distinctive and unforgettable experiences to tourists.

In conclusion, the combination of Yokohama's natural beauty, extensive history, and exciting cultural activities mesmerizes tourists. Every traveler may find something to enjoy in Yokohama, whether they want to take in the city's historical landmarks, beautiful scenery, or lively events.

CHAPTER TWO:
Planning Your Trip to Yokohama

When organizing your trip to Yokohama, you should think about a number of things, including the ideal time to go, the visa and travel requirements, the transit alternatives, the lodging possibilities, and the value of travel insurance. To guarantee a comfortable and enjoyable journey, this chapter will give you comprehensive information on each of these areas.

Best Time to Visit

Your interests and the kind of experience you're looking for will determine the optimum time to visit Yokohama:

- Spring (March to May): Because of the blooming cherry blossoms, spring is a popular time to visit Yokohama. Delicate pink flowers start to cover the city's parks and gardens, including Sankeien Garden and Yamashita Park, providing a lovely scene.

- Autumn (September to November): Another fantastic time to go, particularly if you like the vibrant foliage. This time of year is popular among outdoor enthusiasts due to the pleasant weather and colorful autumn foliage in parks like Mitsuike Park and Negishi Forest Park.

- Mild Winters (December to February: Yokohama experiences moderate winters, making it an ideal destination for tourists who enjoy colder weather. Winters offer a more serene ambiance and fewer crowds, notwithstanding the possibility of the rare downpour.

Visa and Travel Requirements

Make sure you have the required visas and travel documentation before making travel arrangements to Yokohama. Many nations have visa waiver agreements with Japan, enabling travelers to enter the country without a visa for brief periods. The maximum stay, however, differs depending on nationality.

Citizens of nations with which Japan has visa-free travel arrangements may, for instance, stay in Japan for up to 90 days. Even for brief trips, some nationalities may need a visa. It is imperative to confirm the exact visa requirements for your nation on the embassy or consulate of Japan's official website.

How to Get There

Yokohama is easily reachable from several locations in Japan and the rest of the world:

- By Air: If you're flying in from abroad, Tokyo Haneda Airport (HND), which handles both domestic and international flights, is the closest significant airport. You can quickly go to Yokohama from Haneda Airport by airport limousine bus or by riding the Tokyo Monorail to Hamamatsucho Station and changing to a train headed that direction.

- By Train: From Tokyo Station, you can take a Shinkansen (bullet train) to Yokohama if you are already in Japan. It takes about 25 minutes to travel.

- By Bus: Travelers have the option of taking long-distance buses to get from Yokohama to a number of cities in Japan at a reasonable price.

Getting Around

Yokohama has a comprehensive and effective public transportation system that makes getting about the city simple:

- Trains: The Japan Railways (JR) and Yokohama Municipal Subway lines provide access to most of the city. The Tokyu Toyoko Line and the Minato Mirai Line make it simple to reach well-known tourist destinations.

- Buses: Yokohama's bus network is a handy addition to the rail network and is especially helpful for traveling to locations that are not easily accessible by train.

- Taxis: Although they are widely accessible, taxis can be pricey when compared to other modes of transportation.

Accommodations Options

Yokohama provides a variety of lodging choices to accommodate all tastes and price ranges:

1. Luxury Hotels: The Yokohama Bay Hotel Tokyu and the InterContinental Yokohama Grand are two outstanding choices for guests looking for first-rate amenities and first-rate service.

2. Business Hotels: Business hotels with inexpensive prices include the APA Hotel Yokohama-Kannai and the Daiwa Roynet Hotel Yokohama-Koen.

3. Ryokans: Experience traditional Japanese hospitality by staying in a ryokan, like the Yokohama Minato Mirai Manyo Club, which provides a taste of Japanese culture with tatami rooms and onsen (hot spring) baths.

4. Hostels: Budget travelers can opt for hostels like the Yokohama Hostel Village Hayashi-Kaikan, offering affordable dormitory-style accommodations.

Sample Accommodation Options:

1. Yokohama Royal Park Hotel: A luxurious hotel located in the Minato Mirai area, offering stunning views of the city and bay. The hotel features elegant rooms, a spa, and several dining options.

2. Yokohama Central Hostel: A cozy and budget-friendly hostel with both dormitory and private rooms. It's centrally located, making it easy to explore Yokohama's attractions.

3. Hotel New Grand: A historic hotel with a blend of Western and Japanese architecture, providing a charming and nostalgic ambiance. It's conveniently situated near Yamashita Park and Yokohama Chinatown.

Travel Insurance

To safeguard yourself against unforeseen events while traveling, purchase travel insurance. It ought to cover unexpected medical costs, trip interruptions, misplaced or delayed baggage, and other travel-related occurrences. Review the policy in detail and select the level of protection that best fits your needs and plans while visiting Yokohama.

You can guarantee a memorable and stress-free trip to Yokohama, Japan, by taking these factors into account and making the appropriate plans. Travel safely!

CHAPTER THREE:
Yokohama's Top Attractions

The city of Yokohama is teeming with alluring landmarks that highlight its extensive past, thriving culture, and cutting-edge growth. We will examine five must-see sights in Yokohama in this chapter.

Yokohama Chinatown

One of the biggest and liveliest Chinatowns in the world is in Yokohama. This thriving neighborhood, which is in the center of the city, is a mash-up of Chinese culture, cuisine, and traditions. Ornate gates, a sea of vivid red lanterns, and a buzzing atmosphere will meet you as you enter Chinatown.

Key Highlights:

- Kanteibyo Temple: A magnificent Chinese temple honoring the Chinese sea goddess Mazu with elaborate decorations.

- Yokohama Daisekai: A vibrant shopping and entertainment center with a recognizable red gate that houses a variety of stores and eateries.

- Chinese Cuisine: Discover the many gastronomic delights of Chinatown, from Peking duck and other local specialties to traditional dim sum and dumplings.

Minato Mirai 21

The sleek waterfront neighborhood of Minato Mirai 21, also known as "Port of the Future 21," symbolizes the futuristic side of Yokohama. It is a center for dining, shopping, entertainment, and stunning architecture. The region is the ideal fusion of modern urban development and beautiful waterfront views.

Key Highlights:

- Landmark Tower: One of Japan's highest structures, the Landmark Tower is home to a posh hotel as well as offices, retail stores, and restaurants. Additionally, it has a "Sky Garden" observation deck with breath-taking panoramic views of Yokohama and beyond.

- Cosmo Clock 21: Located in the Cosmo World theme park, this enormous Ferris wheel serves as a representation of Minato Mirai and offers breathtaking views of the city at night.

- Red Brick Warehouse: Formerly a customs complex, the Red Brick Warehouse is now a shopping center featuring distinctive shops, galleries, and restaurants.

Sankeien Garden

The lovely Sankeien Garden is a traditional Japanese garden that captures the splendor of each season. This tranquil haven is about 175,000 square meters in size and includes tranquil tea houses, historically significant structures, and carefully planned landscapes.

Key Highlights:
- Historic Houses: The garden is home to a number of old wooden buildings that have been moved from various parts of Japan, including pagodas, tea houses, and samurai dwellings.

- Seasonal Beauty: Visitors can see the blooming cherry blossoms in the spring or the vivid autumn foliage in the fall, depending on the season.

- Tea Ceremony: Participate in the customary Japanese tea ceremony in a real tea house tucked away in the garden.

Yamashita Park

Yamashita Park is a well-liked waterfront park that spans along Yokohama Bay and provides a lovely combination of natural beauty and ocean vistas. It is a well-liked location for residents and visitors to unwind, take a leisurely stroll, and take in the adjacent attractions.

Key Highlights:

- Hikawa Maru: A repurposed ocean liner that now serves as a museum ship, it gives tourists a look at its opulent interiors and maritime heritage.

- Statue of the Girl with Red Shoes: A charming bronze statue symbolizing hope and recovery, which holds a special place in the hearts of the people of Yokohama.

Landmark Tower and Sky Garden

The Landmark Tower is a well-known skyscraper and an important landmark of the city's skyline in Yokohama. The tower contains a number of amenities, including an opulent hotel, offices, retail stores, and restaurants. The Sky

Garden, an observation deck on the 69th floor, is the main attraction, though.

Key Highlights:

- Sky Garden: The Sky Garden is a must-see location, especially at sunset and in the evening when the city lights create a stunning show. It offers unrivaled panoramic views of Yokohama, Tokyo, and Mount Fuji.

- Restaurants and Shopping: The Landmark Tower is home to several eateries and shops where guests may splurge on great meals and discover one-of-a-kind mementos.

These top attractions provide tourists a sense of Yokohama's rich history, cultural legacy, and contemporary allure while showcasing the diversity and attractiveness of the city. Every one of these locations guarantees a special and unforgettable experience that will have an impact on your trip to Yokohama.

CHAPTER FOUR:
Yokohama's Cultural Heritage

The cultural heritage of Yokohama is a reflection of the city's long history, global influences, and artistic accomplishments. This chapter will examine five prominent cultural sites that honor the rich tradition and creative diversity of Yokohama.

Yokohama Museum of Art

The Yokohama Museum of Art is a prominent cultural institution that showcases a wide range of contemporary and traditional artworks. The museum's building is a work of art with a contemporary design by architect Kenzo Tange, and it is situated in the Minato Mirai 21 neighborhood. Inside, there is a varied collection of Japanese and Western art, as well as recurring shows by artists from throughout the world.

Key Highlights:

- Permanent Collection: The museum's permanent collection consists of contemporary art installations, 19th- and 20th-century Western art, and Japanese modern art.

- Exhibitions: Throughout the year, the museum holds a number of exhibitions that cover a wide range of artistic genres and topics.

- Art Library and Workshops: Clients may use the art library for research purposes and take part in workshops and educational activities.

Yokohama Red Brick Warehouse

The Yokohama Red Brick Warehouse, which was initially built as customs buildings in the early 20th century, is now a cultural complex that protects its authentic appeal. The warehouses have been modernized and used as offices, stores, galleries, and event locations. The waterfront location of the Red Brick Warehouse provides lovely views of the bay.

Key Highlights:

- Shopping and Dining: The building complex is home to a number of shops, including boutiques, craft shops, and gift shops. Restaurants and cafes with waterfront views are also available for visitors to enjoy.

- Cultural Events: The Red Brick Warehouse presents seasonal festivals, art exhibits, and cultural events all year long.

Yokohama Port Museum

The Port Museum in Yokohama, a city with a long maritime history, provides information about the growth and importance of the city's port. The museum offers a fascinating tour through Yokohama's past as a thriving international port with interactive exhibitions, historical artifacts, and ship models.

Key Highlights:
- Historical Exhibits: The museum depicts the development of maritime trade, the opening of Yokohama's port to foreign trade, and the impact of global communities.

- Ship Models: Visitors can get an insight into historical maritime transportation through intricate models of historic ships and vessels.

- Hands-On Activities: The museum provides interactive activities for both kids and adults, including courses on knot-tying and utilizing simulators to navigate ships.

Yokohama Noh Theater

The Yokohama Noh Theater is a cultural treasure for anybody with an interest in traditional Japanese performing arts. The theater offers a genuine setting to appreciate this ancient art form. Noh is a traditional Japanese musical drama that dates back to the 14th century.

Key Highlights:

- Noh Performances: The theater often presents Noh plays, in which seasoned performers perform age-old dramas to the accompaniment of live music and chanting.

- Traditional Architecture: The structure's design is based on traditional Japanese architecture, giving the performances an authentic setting.

- Workshops and Events: To acquaint guests with the nuances of Noh, the theater occasionally hosts workshops and events.

Yokohama Silk Museum

One of the main trading commodities in Yokohama's early years of international trade was silk, which had a huge impact on the city's history. The Yokohama Silk Museum honors this tradition and offers details on the production of silk as well as its cultural significance.

Key Highlights:

- Silk-Making Process: The museum displays the complete silk production process, from the spinning of silkworms' cocoons through the weaving of the finished silk cloth.

- Historical items: In addition to exhibits on silk crafts and traditional Japanese silk clothing, visitors can examine historical items connected to silk production and trading.

- Hands-On Activities: The museum provides interactive activities that let visitors get a close-up look at the creation of silk. Examples include workshops for spinning and weaving silk.

These Yokohama landmarks offer educational opportunities that emphasize the artistic prowess, maritime history, and traditional performing arts of the area. Immerse yourself in Yokohama's cultural diversity to better understand the city's complex character.

CHAPTER FIVE:
Exploring Yokohama's Neighborhoods

Each of Yokohama's neighborhoods has its own unique personality and allure, providing tourists with a wide range of experiences. In this chapter, we will delve into five of the city's neighborhoods: Yokohama Bay Area, Yokohama Station Area, Yokohama Stadium and Chinatown, Motomachi and Yamate, and Kannai and Noge.

Kannai and Noge

The historical center of Yokohama, Kannai, is renowned for its entertainment and cultural activities. It is the location of numerous significant landmarks, museums, and theaters. With so much action going on nearby, Kannai

Station is a great place to start your exploration of Yokohama.

Key Highlights in Kannai:

- Yokohama facility: The Yokohama DeNA BayStars call Yokohama Stadium their home field. It is a well-known baseball facility. Along with concerts, it also holds other events.

-Yokohama Silk Museum: As previously noted, this museum examines Yokohama's silk origins and presents interesting exhibits on the process of creating silk.

- Yokohama Creative City Center (YCC): An institution for contemporary art that presents performances, workshops, and exhibitions to highlight the creative spirit of the community.

- Noge: is a trendy neighborhood located to the west of Kannai. It has a more laid-back and bohemian atmosphere, attracting a younger crowd with its unique shops, cafes, and izakayas (Japanese pubs).

Key Highlights in Noge:

- Noge Street: The bustling and artistic atmosphere of Noge is reflected in the street's wonderful cafes, pubs, and vintage stores.

- Noge Tatsuya: This well-known jazz venue in the region draws both regional and foreign jazz players.

Motomachi and Yamate

The trendy and upscale neighborhood of Motomachi combines European and Japanese influences. It has broad streets lined with upscale stores, hip cafes, and eateries, making it a well-liked location for dining and shopping.

Key Highlights in Motomachi:

- Motomachi Shopping Street: A bustling street with a mix of local stores and foreign brands, providing a great shopping experience.

- Motomachi Park: A serene sanctuary with cherry blossom trees that offers a peaceful setting for picnics and relaxation.

• Yamate: Yamate is an upscale residential area located on a hill overlooking Yokohama Bay. It has a distinct foreign influence, with elegant Western-style houses and lush greenery.

Key Highlights in Yamate:

- Yamate 111 Bankan: A former residence in the Western style that now houses a museum displaying the culture and architecture of the Yamate region.

- Harbor View Park: A wonderful park with sweeping views of the city skyline and Yokohama Bay.

Yokohama Bay Area

A contemporary and international neighborhood, the Yokohama Bay Area is renowned for its iconic skyline, waterfront attractions, and exciting entertainment.

Key Highlights in Yokohama Bay Area:

- Minato Mirai 21: The futuristic cityscape of Minato Mirai 21 is filled with skyscrapers, shopping malls, and entertainment complexes like the Landmark Tower and Red Brick Warehouse.

- Cosmo World: An amusement park including exhilarating rides, such as the renowned Cosmo Clock 21 Ferris wheel.

- PACIFICO Yokohama: A convention center that offers a variety of activities, including shows and concerts.

Yokohama Station Area

A thriving transit hub and commercial area with a variety of places to eat, shop, and have fun is known as the Yokohama Station Area.

Key Highlights in Yokohama Station Area:

- Sogo Yokohama: A sizable department store with several levels of clothing, beauty products, and home furnishings.

- Yokohama Takashimaya: Another upscale department store with a wide selection of luxury products and gourmet dining selections is the Yokohama Takashimaya.

- Yokohama Bay Quarter: A cutting-edge mall with a theater, eateries, and stores.

Yokohama Stadium and Chinatown

The Yokohama Stadium and Chinatown neighborhood offers a unique fusion of sporting events, cultural attractions, and mouthwatering cuisine.

Key Highlights in Yokohama Stadium and Chinatown:

- Yokohama Stadium: As previously noted, the stadium holds baseball games and other events, creating a buzz for sports fans.

- Yokohama Chinatown: A thriving and busy neighborhood with a wide variety of Chinese eateries, stores, and cultural activities. It offers a wide selection of mouthwatering Chinese cuisine, making it a food lover's delight.

Visitors can experience the multidimensional nature of Yokohama, from its historical origins to its recent advancements, and can appreciate the city's rich cultural legacy and active urban life by exploring these diverse areas. Every traveler may find something to enjoy in Yokohama's neighborhoods, whether they are interested in history, shopping, cuisine, or entertainment.

CHAPTER SIX:
Yokohama's Culinary Scene

The culinary scene in Yokohama is a culinary journey that features a delicious blend of traditional Japanese flavors, foreign influences, and a thriving street food culture. Yokohama provides a wide variety of appetizing foods that would satisfy any culinary enthusiast, from fine seafood and sushi to hearty ramen, delicious yakitori, and locally brewed craft beer and sake. We will examine the gastronomic high points of Yokohama in this chapter, offering a thorough guide to enjoying the greatest cuisine the city has to offer.

Traditional Japanese Cuisine

With access to seasonal fresh ingredients from the nearby ocean and surrounding farmlands, Yokohama's chefs take pride in creating dishes that emphasize simplicity, balance, and natural flavors.

Key Traditional Dishes in Yokohama:

- Tempura: Yokohama residents and tourists alike appreciate this delectable dish made of fish, veggies, and mushrooms that have been lightly battered and deep-fried. The batter develops a crispy, golden texture, preserving the ingredients' original flavors.

- Sukiyaki: A hearty hot pot dish made with tofu, veggies, thinly sliced beef, and shirataki noodles simmered in a sweet soy broth. The finest time to eat sukiyaki is in the winter.

- Chawanmushi: A delicate and savory steamed egg custard with a variety of ingredients like chicken, shrimp, mushrooms, and ginkgo nuts.

- Nabe: A variety of Japanese hot pot dishes made with tofu, vegetables, fish, meat, and other items cooked in a delicious broth.

Yokohama Ramen

It is impossible to fully experience Yokohama's cuisine without indulging in some of its world-famous ramen. Despite having its roots in China, ramen has evolved into a staple of Japanese cuisine, with each region claiming its own distinct style. Ramen from Yokohama is distinctive for its flavorful broth made with pork and its thin, straight noodles.

Key Ramen Varieties in Yokohama:

- Ie-kei Ramen: Ie-kei ramen is a specialty of Yokohama and is distinguished by its creamy tonkotsu (pork bone) broth and a mix of medium-thick and thin noodles. Roasted pork, cooked spinach, and seasoned bamboo shoots are common toppings.

- Shina Soba: A clear broth, salt-based ramen with slices of roast pork, green onions, and nori (seaweed) on top, is a dish with Chinese culinary influences.

- Tonkotsu Ramen: Although not unique to Yokohama, this variety of ramen is known for its milky, collagen-rich broth, which is created by boiling pork bones for many hours to give the soup a velvety feel.

Seafood and Sushi

Yokohama, which is close to the huge Tokyo Bay, has a plentiful supply of fresh fish. As a result, sushi and seafood dishes constitute an essential aspect of the city's cuisine.

Key Seafood Dishes and Sushi in Yokohama:
- Sushi: Yokohama's sushi establishments take great delight in offering top-notch, seasonal fish. The region's sushi selection is extensive, ranging from traditional nigiri (fish on rice) to innovative contemporary rolls.

- Sashimi: Enjoy a variety of fresh sashimi, which is made up of raw fish or other seafood that has been thinly sliced and is carefully placed on a platter.

- Kaisen Don: A delicious rice bowl garnished with a variety of sashimi and seafood, such as tuna, salmon, octopus, shrimp, and more.

- Grilled Fish: You may get a variety of grilled fish meals in izakayas and restaurants. Seafood is seasoned and cooked over charcoal for a delicious smoky flavor.

Izakayas and Yakitori

Izakayas are traditional Japanese bars where folks congregate to mingle while sipping beers and nibbling on a variety of mouthwatering small plates. In izakayas, skewered and grilled chicken in a variety of cuts and seasonings is known as "yakitori," or "yakitori."

Key Highlights of Izakayas and Yakitori in Yokohama:

- Yakitori: Try a variety of yakitori skewers, including juicy chicken meatballs, crispy skin on chicken, succulent chicken thighs, and other delectable selections, frequently coated with a savory tare (sauce).

- Izakaya Specialties: In addition to yakitori, izakayas provide a wide range of small plates and appetizers, including edamame, takoyaki, karaage, and gyoza.

- Nomihodai and Tabehodai: Some izakayas include "nomihodai" (all-you-can-drink) and "tabehodai" (all-you-can-eat) options for a set fee, enabling customers to indulge in a wide range of foods and drinks.

Yokohama Craft Beer and Sake

For fans of beer and sake, Yokohama has a thriving craft beer culture and a long history of sake making.

Key Highlights of Craft Beer and Sake in Yokohama:

- Craft Beer: There are several craft breweries in the city that offer a wide variety of brews, from IPAs that are incredibly hoppy to creamy stouts. Popular locations to sample regionally brewed beer include the Bashamichi Taproom and the Yokohama Craft Beer Market in Kannai.

- Sake: Brewing sake has a long history in Yokohama and is still a significant aspect of the city's culture. Visitors can tour nearby breweries and sample several kinds of sake, from dry to sweet.

- Sake Tasting: Many sake breweries in Yokohama provide guided tours and sake tasting opportunities, enabling guests to discover the process of manufacturing sake and sample many varieties.

The food scene in Yokohama is a wonderful tour of Japanese flavors and customs with a dash of foreign influence. Yokohama guarantees a memorable and mouthwatering experience for every palate, whether you are savoring traditional Japanese cuisine, indulging in a bowl of piping hot ramen, savoring the freshness of seafood and sushi, savoring the grilled delights of izakayas, or raising a glass of craft beer or sake. The city's culinary inventiveness and legacy make it a veritable haven for foodies looking to discover the heart of Japanese cuisine.

CHAPTER SEVEN:
Hidden Gems in Yokohama

There are many well-known sites in Yokohama, a city with a dynamic modern culture and a long past. It does, however, contain a number of undiscovered treasures that provide uncommon and off-the-beaten-path experiences for tourists looking for something unusual. We will examine five of Yokohama's undiscovered attractions in this chapter, including the Yamate Italian Garden, Orbi Yokohama, Shomyo-ji Temple, Yokohama Curry Museum, and Nogeyama Zoo. These undiscovered gems offer a window into the city's lesser-known but no less fascinating features, making them must-see locations for adventurous travelers.

Yamate Italian Garden

The Yamate Italian Garden, tucked away in the Yamate neighborhood, is a magical haven that whisks tourists away to the breathtaking vistas of Italy. The fact that Yamate was formerly a neighborhood for foreign diplomats and traders during the Meiji era is a tribute to the city's global heritage.

Key Highlights of Yamate Italian Garden:

- Italian Architecture: Take in the garden's European-inspired architecture as you stroll through it, which includes a lovely pavilion covered in roses and a quaint tea house.

- Seasonal Beauty: The garden's beauty varies with the seasons, including cherry blossoms in the spring, lush vegetation in the summer, and vivid foliage in the fall.

- Panoramic Views: From various vantage points within the garden, take in breathtaking panoramic views of Yokohama's port and metropolis.

Orbi Yokohama

Orbi Yokohama is a hidden gem that combines the best of technology and nature. Created in collaboration with the BBC and Sega, this unique attraction takes visitors on an immersive and interactive journey through the natural world.

Key Highlights of Orbi Yokohama:

- Sensory Experience: Using cutting-edge technology, Orbi provides a multisensory experience with 3D projection mapping, high-definition images, and surround sound.

- Interactive Exhibits: Participate in interactive displays that let visitors get up close and personal with a variety of animals and ecosystems, from the vast savannah to the ocean's depths.

- Educational and Entertaining: Orbi is a great place for families and nature lovers to visit because of its compelling presentations, which are both instructive and entertaining.

Shomyo-ji Temple

The Shomyo-ji Temple, which is tucked away in the peaceful Koganecho area, is a hidden gem that offers a tranquil retreat from the busy metropolis. This ancient temple, which dates back to the 13th century, provides a window into the spiritual and cultural history of Yokohama.

Key Highlights of Shomyo-ji Temple:
- Beautiful Garden: The temple grounds have a magnificent Japanese garden with carefully tended gardens, tranquil ponds, and conventional stone lanterns.

- Peaceful Atmosphere: Enjoy a calm environment away from the throng where you can unwind, practice meditation, and think.

- Seasonal Events: Shomyo-ji Temple hosts special occasions throughout the year, including viewings of the cherry blossoms in the spring and the fall foliage.

Yokohama Curry Museum

Even though curry might not be the first food that springs to mind when considering the cuisine of Yokohama, the city has a special fondness for this savory dish. The "Yokohama Curry Museum," a hidden gem that honors the curry world's diversity, is located in the Shin-Yokohama neighborhood.

Key Highlights of Yokohama Curry Museum:
- Curry History: Discover the origins of curry in Yokohama and how it has changed through the years in response to various influences.

- Curry Tasting: The museum offers a curry buffet with a variety of curry flavors from many locations and cultures, allowing visitors to sample and contrast different kinds.

- Curry Souvenirs: Buy trinkets and things related to curry for one-of-a-kind gifts to send home.

Nogeyama Zoo

The Nogeyama Zoo is a hidden jewel that provides a lovely escape into the animal realm, and it is located in Nogeyama Park, tucked away on a hill. Despite being smaller than other zoos, it offers visitors a charming and personal experience.

Key Highlights of Nogeyama Zoo:

- Animal Encounters: Get up close with a variety of animals, including red pandas, meerkats, capybaras, and more.

- Petting Area: The zoo offers a petting area where guests can get up close and personal with little animals, making it a popular destination for families with kids.

- Picnic Spots: Nogeyama Park, which is adjacent to the zoo, is a beautiful location for a picnic with lovely vistas and peaceful greenery.

The undiscovered gems of Yokohama offer a novel and genuine view of the city that extends beyond its well-known attractions. These hidden gems offer one-of-a-kind experiences that add depth and richness to any trip to Yokohama, whether it's relaxing in the serene atmosphere of the Yamate Italian Garden, taking in the natural wonders at Orbi Yokohama, discovering the historical serenity of Shomyo-ji Temple, indulging in the diverse world of curry at the Yokohama Curry Museum, or having a close encounter with animals at Nogeyama Zoo. Embrace your inner explorer and go off-the-beaten-path to find the city's lesser-known but no less fascinating hidden gems.

CHAPTER EIGHT:
Outdoor Activities in Yokohama

With its scenic bay region and beautiful surroundings, Yokohama provides a wide range of outdoor activities to suit different interests and tastes. This chapter will explore five exhilarating outdoor activities in Yokohama that enable tourists to embrace nature, experience excitement, and make lifelong memories. These activities range from picturesque parks and tranquil coastal promenades to daring island explorations and marine adventures.

Yamashita Park and Seaside Promenade

Located on the waterfront and with views of Yokohama Bay, Yamashita Park is one of Yokohama's most popular open areas. This large park is a well-liked hangout for both locals and tourists, providing a lovely blend of vegetation, ocean views, and recreational activities.

Key Highlights of Yamashita Park and Seaside Promenade:

- Scenic Strolls: Enjoy the views of the harbor, Yokohama Marine Tower, and Osanbashi Pier while taking a leisurely stroll along the promenade.

- Rose Garden: Yamashita Park has a beautiful rose garden with a range of vibrant blossoms, making a nice setting for a leisurely afternoon.

- Cultural Attractions: Check out the Yokohama Doll Museum and the converted ocean liner Hikawa Maru.

Jogashima Island

Jogashima Island is the perfect getaway from the bustle of the city for nature lovers and adventurers. At the southernmost point of the Miura Peninsula, this wild and picturesque island offers beautiful coastal vistas and a wide variety of animals.

Key Highlights of Jogashima Island:

- Hiking and Nature Walks: Set out on charming hiking paths that take you to breathtaking vistas overlooking the Pacific Ocean. The island is well known for both its bright flora and unusual rock structures.

- Fishing and Seafood: Jogashima is a well-known fishing location, and guests can sample delicious fresh seafood dishes in neighborhood restaurants.

- Lighthouse: Visit the Jogashima Lighthouse, which is located at the point of the island and offers sweeping views of the sea and the surrounding area.

Hakkeijima Sea Paradise

The marine-themed amusement park and aquarium complex **Hakkeijima Sea Paradise** guarantees a day of adventure and aquatic exploration. This large attraction, which is located on an artificial island in Yokohama Bay, is ideal for families and ocean lovers.

Key Highlights of Hakkeijima Sea Paradise:

- Aqua Resorts and Aquariums: The park consists of four distinct areas, including Aqua Resort, Dolphin Fantasy, Fureai Lagoon, and Umi Farm. Each area offers a unique marine experience, including dolphin and sea lion shows, touch pools, and interactive exhibits.

- Thrilling Rides: Experience heart-pounding thrills on the Surf Coaster, an exhilarating roller coaster with thrilling twists and turns, and the Blue Fall, an exhilarating drop tower that plunges you toward the water.

- Spectacular Night Aquarium: In the evening, illuminations and a magnificent "Night Aquarium" experience transform the tanks into a mystical world.

Mitsuike Park

In the heart of Yokohama's urban setting, Mitsuike Park is a calm haven. This large park is a great place to unwind and engage in outdoor activities thanks to its tranquil ponds, lush vegetation, and various flora.

Key Highlights of Mitsuike Park:

- Walking and Cycling Trails: Mitsuike Park offers walking and cycling paths that wind through the park's natural landscapes, making it a popular destination for outdoor enthusiasts.

- Cherry Blossom Viewing: In the spring, as the cherry blossoms bloom, the park transforms into a picturesque wonderland, drawing tourists for customary hanami (flower-viewing) picnics.

- Seasonal Attractions: The park holds a number of events and seasonal attractions throughout the year, such as holiday light displays.

Yokohama Cosmo World

Yokohama Cosmo World is a thriving entertainment center located close to Yokohama Bay and offers exhilarating amusement park experiences for anyone looking for them. This urban theme park provides a variety of traditional rides, contemporary attractions, and breathtaking nighttime views.

Key Highlights of Yokohama Cosmo World:
- Cosmo Clock 21: The well-known Cosmo Clock 21 Ferris wheel is a well-known landmark of Yokohama and provides stunning views of the city and bay, particularly when lit up at night.

- Roller Coasters and Rides: The park offers a variety of rides and roller coasters that are appropriate for all ages and offer the ideal combination of thrill and fun.

- Wonder Amuse Zone: A specially designated area for small children, with moderate rides and fascinating activities.

The outdoor activities in Yokohama offer a wide variety of experiences that are suitable for people of all ages and interests. The city offers the ideal blend of urban delights and natural wonders, from the tranquil beauty of Yamashita Park and Seaside Promenade to the exhilarating adventures of Jogashima Island and Hakkeijima Sea Paradise, and the unhurried charm of Mitsuike Park and adrenaline of Yokohama

Cosmo World. The outdoor attractions in Yokohama are sure to leave you with treasured memories and amazing experiences, whether you're looking for recreation, adventure, marine discovery, or entertainment. Enjoy the great outdoors and everything that Yokohama's varied and exciting outdoor offerings have to offer.

CHAPTER NINE:
Shopping and Souvenirs in Yokohama

Visitors can enjoy a wide variety of fascinating retail experiences in Yokohama, a shopping heaven. This chapter will examine six important shopping areas in Yokohama, ranging from contemporary retail malls and traditional markets to quaint shopping lanes. To assist visitors get the most out of their shopping outings and locate the ideal trinkets to bring home that capture the spirit of this energetic city, we'll also offer shopping advice.

Yokohama World Porters

In the Minato Mirai 21 neighborhood, Yokohama World Porters is a cutting-edge retail center with a range of stores, restaurants, and entertainment venues. European architecture served as the inspiration for the distinctive design of this mall, which gives it a welcoming atmosphere.

Shopping Highlights at Yokohama World Porters:

- Fashion Boutiques: Look through a variety of fashion boutiques that sell stylish apparel, accessories, and shoes for people of all ages.

- Specialty Stores: Look around specialized shops that sell toys, gadgets, cosmetics, and other household goods.

- Gourmet Dining: Choose from a variety of cafes and restaurants serving anything from Japanese to cosmopolitan delicacies.

Yokohama Landmark Plaza

In the Minato Mirai 21 neighborhood, close to the Yokohama Landmark Tower, lies the premium shopping center known as **Yokohama Landmark Plaza**. This mall caters to individuals looking for high-end shopping experiences with its opulent environment and high-end stores.

Shopping Highlights at Yokohama Landmark Plaza:

- Luxury Brands: Explore a variety of luxury brands that offer designer apparel, jewelry, and accessories.

- Gourmet Delights: Discover a variety of premium eateries and gourmet food shops, ideal for indulging in mouthwatering culinary delights.

- Sky Garden Observatory: For stunning city views after shopping, climb to the 69th story of the Yokohama Landmark Tower's Sky Garden Observatory.

Yokohama AkaRenga Soko

Yokohama AkaRenga Soko, commonly referred to as Red Brick Warehouse, is a famous shopping center from the first half of the 20th century. Originally utilized as customs warehouses, the structures have been renovated into a commercial and cultural hub.

Shopping Highlights at Yokohama AkaRenga Soko:

- Arts and Crafts: Browse a variety of stores that offer handmade goods, arts and crafts, and one-of-a-kind souvenirs.

- Cafes and Restaurants: Relish a meal or a cup of coffee at one of the quaint cafes or restaurants that look out over the water.

- Events and Festivals: The Red Brick Warehouse holds a number of cultural events, craft fairs, and seasonal festivals all year long.

Yokohama Bay Quarter

Yokohama Bay Quarter is a modern shopping and entertainment complex located in the Minato Mirai 21 area. With its striking architecture and waterfront location, this mall offers a trendy shopping experience.

Shopping Highlights at Yokohama Bay Quarter:

- Fashion and Lifestyle Stores: Shop for fashionable clothing, accessories, and lifestyle goods from various popular brands.

- Cinema and Entertainment: Attend entertainment events at the location or watch the newest films in the nearby theater.

- Dining by the Bay: Indulge in delectable meals at eateries that provide breathtaking views of Yokohama Bay.

Yokohama Motomachi Shopping Street

Yamate and Motomachi areas are close to the lovely and historic shopping street known as "Yokohama Motomachi Shopping Street." This busy street has a mix of traditional and modern stores, making it a great location to learn about the local way of life and purchase one-of-a-kind gifts.

Shopping Highlights at Yokohama Motomachi Shopping Street:

- Traditional Shops: Explore stores with a long history that sell kimonos, traditional crafts, and Japanese sweets.

- Fashion Boutiques: Discover chic stores that feature a blend of Japanese and international style.

- Cafes and Snack Stands: Sample delicious delights at a variety of cafes, bakeries, and snack stalls.

Shopping Tips:

1. Tax-Free Shopping: Shoppers from outside of Japan can shop tax-free at several establishments in Yokohama. Keep an eye out for "Tax-Free" signs, and don't forget to show the cashier your passport.

2. Credit Cards and Cash: Major credit cards are widely accepted in shopping malls and large stores. However, it's a good idea to carry some cash, especially when shopping in smaller local shops or street markets.

3. Opening Hours: The majority of Yokohama's shops are open from about 10:00 AM to 8:00

PM. But certain stores in popular tourist regions might operate longer hours.

4. Seasonal Sales: Keep an eye out for seasonal sales, particularly around the New Year, throughout the Golden Week, and at end-of-season clearance sales.

5. Souvenir Ideas: Consider buying green tea, specialty local snacks, traditional apparel, Japanese crafts, traditional accessories, or distinctive local foods as keepsakes.

6. Bring a Reusable Bag: To cut down on trash, several establishments charge for disposable bags. The use of reusable bags can be practical and environmentally friendly.

7. Language Assistance: Even though major shopping centers may have English signage, knowing a few fundamental Japanese words and phrases can be useful, especially when browsing local markets.

Shopping in Yokohama is varied, fascinating, and catered to all tastes and inclinations. Visitors can explore a variety of shopping locations that reflect the city's dynamic and cosmopolitan spirit, from contemporary shopping centers like Yokohama World Porters and Yokohama Landmark Plaza to historic landmarks like Yokohama AkaRenga Soko and charming streets like Yokohama Motomachi Shopping Street. Follow the shopping advice to get the most out of your outings, and don't forget to bring home one-of-a-kind trinkets that perfectly express the beauty and colorful culture of Yokohama. Enjoy your shopping!

CHAPTER TEN:
Nightlife and Entertainment in Yokohama

For both locals and tourists, Yokohama's thriving nightlife and entertainment industry offers a wide variety of activities. This chapter will dig into the intriguing world of Yokohama's nightlife and entertainment alternatives, from hip bars and buzzing clubs to soulful jazz bars and cultural shows. Yokohama offers plenty to offer everyone's tastes, whether you're looking for a night of dancing and mingling with friends or a sophisticated evening of music and culture.

Bars and Clubs in Kannai

The busy Kannai neighborhood, Yokohama's historic center, is well-known for its exciting nightlife and entertainment alternatives. A diverse selection of taverns, clubs, and pubs that appeal to all interests and preferences fill the streets.

Key Highlights of Bars and Clubs in Kannai:

- Pub Crawls: Experience Kannai's thriving bar scene by going on a pub crawl. A variety of domestic and foreign beers and spirits are available in many establishments.

- Dance Clubs: Enjoy a night of dancing at one of the many clubs that offer DJs, live music, and a fun atmosphere.

- Izakayas: Visit neighborhood izakayas (Japanese pubs) for a more authentic experience and savor a selection of delectable dishes and drinks.

Jazz Bars in Noge

Noge, located to the west of Kannai, is a trendy and bohemian neighborhood known for its love for jazz music. The area is dotted with cozy jazz bars that offer a unique and soulful ambiance.

Key Highlights of Jazz Bars in Noge:

- Live Performances: Take in a live jazz concert by a group of skilled neighborhood musicians. Some pubs may also host special appearances by well-known performers.

- Intimate Setting: Jazz bars in Noge frequently provide a warm, intimate atmosphere that makes for the perfect place to relax and take in the music.

- Cultural Experience: Noge, with its love of jazz music, provides a rich cultural experience for jazz fans.

Yokohama Symphony Orchestra

The Yokohama Symphony Orchestra offers world-class musical performances for fans of classical music. Since its founding in 1967, the orchestra has won praise for its outstanding performances on a global scale.

Key Highlights of Yokohama Symphony Orchestra:

- Concerts and Performances: Attend classical performances featuring well-known soloists, conductors, and works from diverse musical eras.

- Yokohama Minato Mirai Hall: The majority of the orchestra's performances take place at this stunning concert venue, which also has exceptional acoustics.

- Educational Programs: To encourage a love of classical music among the younger generation, the orchestra offers educational programs and activities.

Music Venues Live

Numerous live music venues in Yokohama offer a wide range of musical styles. These venues provide a stage for both established and up-and-coming performers in genres ranging from rock and pop to independent and alternative.

Key Live Music Venues in Yokohama:

- Bay Hall: Located in Minato Mirai, Bay Hall presents a variety of concerts, including rock, pop, jazz, and classical performances.

- Thumbs Up: A well-known live-music venue in Yokohama that prides itself on promoting independent and underground acts.

- Club 24: A venue for live music events, DJ sets, and club nights, Club 24 is located in the center of Kannai.

Yokohama Cinema Scene

In Yokohama, there is a vibrant and fascinating film scene for moviegoers. The city has a variety of contemporary multiplex theaters and independent movie theaters that play a variety of films from both Japan and other countries.

Key Highlights of Yokohama Cinema Scene:

- Multiplex Theaters: See a variety of Japanese and foreign films at contemporary multiplex theaters like MOVIX Yokohama and TOHO Cinemas.

- Cinema Jack and Betty: This independent theater in Noge provides a warm and welcoming atmosphere for watching art-house, vintage, and foreign movies.

- Film Festivals: Throughout the year, Yokohama holds a number of film festivals, including the Yokohama Film Festival and the Yokohama International Women's Film Festival.

Everybody may find something to enjoy in Yokohama's nightlife and entertainment scene, which caters to a wide range of preferences and interests. Yokohama promises a dynamic and satisfying nightlife and entertainment experience, whether you choose to explore the bars and clubs in Kannai, immerse yourself in soulful jazz bars in Noge, witness the mesmerizing performances of the Yokohama Symphony Orchestra, find live music venues, or indulge in the film scene. Accept the vibrant and varied attractions of the city, and allow the allure of Yokohama's nightlife and cultural events to mesmerize you.

CHAPTER ELEVEN:
Yokohama's Maritime History

The growth and importance of the city on a global scale are closely related to Yokohama's maritime heritage. Yokohama, one of Japan's most significant ports, was essential to Japan's opening to the outside world throughout the Meiji era and thereafter. This chapter will examine the Yokohama Port Opening Memorial Hall, the NYK nautical Museum, the Kanagawa Prefectural Museum of Cultural History, the Nippon Maru, and the Yokohama Osanbashi Pier, four significant sites that honor Yokohama's nautical past. These locations provide insightful information about the city's nautical past and explain how it developed from a small fishing community to a thriving international port metropolis.

Yokohama Port Opening Memorial Hall

A major historical landmark that honors the opening of Yokohama's port to foreign trade in 1859 is the Yokohama Port Opening Memorial Hall, popularly referred to as the "Kaigan-dori Park." The building serves as a memorial to the crucial time when Japan abandoned its policy of isolation and started to interact with the rest of the world.

Key Features of Yokohama Port Opening Memorial Hall:

- Red Brick Warehouses: A number of beautifully preserved red brick warehouses that are a throwback to Yokohama's maritime past surround the hall.

- Historical Exhibits: The memorial hall is home to displays and artifacts that trace the development of Yokohama's port and highlight its connections to other countries.

- Open-Air Events: Open-air events, cultural festivals, and meetings frequently take place in the roomy park area surrounding the hall.

NYK Maritime Museum

The Nippon Yusen Kaisha (NYK) shipping firm played a vital part in Japan's maritime history, which is thoroughly explored at the NYK Maritime Museum. One of Japan's oldest and most renowned shipping businesses, NYK was established in 1885.

Key Features of NYK Maritime Museum:

- Historic Ship Models: The museum exhibits elaborate ship models of the ships that were essential to Japan's international relations and maritime trade.

- Interactive Exhibits: Interactive displays and multimedia exhibits offer an entertaining experience while teaching visitors about shipbuilding, navigation, and seafaring.

- Maritime Artifacts: The museum is home to a sizable collection of nautical artifacts, which also includes historical records, ship equipment, and navigational devices.

Kanagawa Prefectural Museum of Cultural History

The Kanagawa Prefectural Museum of Cultural History offers useful insights into Yokohama's entire historical evolution, including its marine connections, although not being solely devoted to maritime history.

Key Features of Kanagawa Prefectural Museum of Cultural History:

- Yokohama and Port History: Specific areas of the museum focus on Yokohama's development as a port city and its relationships with other civilizations.

- Cultural Artifacts: Explore a variety of cultural relics from Yokohama and the neighboring

Kanagawa prefecture, such as traditional crafts, works of art, and historical artifacts.

- Temporary Exhibitions: The museum showcases a variety of transient exhibits, many of which have maritime themes.

Nippon Maru and Yokohama Osanbashi Pier

The historic sailing ship Nippon Maru, which is currently berthed at the Yokohama Osanbashi Pier, serves as a floating museum that lets guests take a trip back in time and experience life on a classic sailing ship.

Key Features of Nippon Maru and Yokohama Osanbashi Pier:

- Nippon Maru: Take a tour of the Nippon Maru and discover more about its past as a training vessel for Japanese naval officers. Discover the exhibitions, decks, and cabins that depict sailor life in the late 19th and early 20th centuries.

- Osanbashi Pier: Located on the waterfront, the Osanbashi Pier in Yokohama offers breathtaking views of the bay and the city skyline. Popular places to take leisurely strolls and enjoy the coastal ambiance are here.

- Events and Festivals: The pier area frequently holds a variety of events, such as festivals with a maritime theme and cultural gatherings.

The intriguing journey of Yokohama's maritime past is a reflection of the city's development, change, and ties with the rest of the world. These historical sites provide a window into the past and shed light on Yokohama's essential role in Japan's opening to the outside world, from the Yokohama Port Opening Memorial Hall honoring the port's founding in 1859 to the NYK Maritime Museum showcasing Japan's major shipping heritage. The Kanagawa Prefectural Museum of Cultural History also gives a more comprehensive overview of Yokohama's general evolution, including its linkages to the sea. The Nippon Maru and Yokohama Osanbashi Pier also provide a chance to board a historic sailing ship and take in the picturesque waterfront for a distinctive nautical experience. Visitors can fully experience the nautical legacy that has defined Yokohama's identity and continues to be an integral part of its dynamic culture by visiting these locations.

CHAPTER TWELVE:
Practical Information for Travelers

When visiting Yokohama, having practical information at your fingertips can enhance your travel experience and ensure a smooth journey. This chapter offers thorough explanations of available modes of transportation, money and currency exchange, etiquette in the local tongue and culture, safety advice, and necessary health and medical services. You may make the most of your time in Yokohama while remaining secure, deferential, and well-prepared all through your journey by becoming familiar with these useful details.

Transportation Options

a) Trains and Subways: Yokohama boasts an efficient and extensive train and subway network that connects the city to nearby areas and Tokyo. The major train operators are JR East, Tokyu Corporation, and Keikyu Corporation.

Use the extensive train and subway network to go around Yokohama and beyond. While the Tokyu and Keikyu lines link Yokohama to nearby cities and Tokyo, the JR East lines offer access to popular tourist destinations. For convenient and cashless transportation on buses, trains, and subways, think about buying a Suica or Pasmo card.

b) Buses: Buses are another option for getting about Yokohama, and they can take you places that trains can't get you to. For touring the city's attractions, there are city buses and tourist loop buses available.

Take a ride on the city buses or the tourist loop buses to see Yokohama at your own pace. The "Akai Kutsu" (Red Shoes) buses, which travel to the main sights, are a well-liked choice for tourists. You can get on and off the buses at the attractions of your choice because they follow a set route.

c) Taxis: Taxis are readily available throughout Yokohama, offering a convenient door-to-door transportation option. Taxi fares are metered, and tipping is not customary in Japan.

Consider using a cab in Yokohama for a more convenient and private travel experience. The roof-mounted, LED "taxi" sign makes taxis easy to spot. Make sure to have your destination's name or address written in Japanese ready to show the driver.

Money and Currency Exchange

a) Currency: The Japanese Yen (JPY) is the official currency of Japan. Since not all businesses accept cards, particularly in smaller shops or traditional markets, it is advisable to carry a combination of cash and credit/debit cards.

Ensure you have Japanese Yen (JPY) with you during your stay in Yokohama. While major establishments accept credit/debit cards, having cash is essential for smaller businesses, local markets, and transportation.

b) Currency Exchange: Banks, some hotels, and major international airports all offer currency exchange services. ATMs are also extensively available, and the majority of them in convenience stores and post offices accept foreign cards.

At the airport or nearby Yokohama banks, you can exchange your native cash into Japanese Yen. Alternatively, you can use your foreign card to withdraw money from ATMs at convenience stores or post offices.

Language and Cultural Etiquette

a) Language: The official language in Yokohama and all of Japan is Japanese. Although English may be spoken in tourist areas, learning a few fundamental Japanese words will aid with communication.

Learn some essential Japanese phrases to ease communication with locals. Simple greetings like "Konnichiwa" (Hello) and "Arigatou gozaimasu" (Thank you) are appreciated and can go a long way in creating positive interactions.

b) Cultural Etiquette: Japan has a strong cultural legacy, as well as deeply revered traditions and manners. Familiarize yourself with some basic cultural norms to show respect during your visit.

Practice common cultural etiquettes such as removing shoes when entering someone's home, using two hands when presenting or receiving items, and avoiding loud conversations on public transport.

Safety Tips and Emergency Contacts

a) Safety Precautions: Although Yokohama is typically a safe city, it is nevertheless important to be aware of your surroundings and possessions when visiting any place. Watch out for your possessions and use caution when in crowded places.

Stay vigilant and be cautious of pickpockets, especially in crowded places like train stations and popular tourist spots. Avoid displaying large sums of money or valuable items in public.

b) Emergency Contacts: Knowing the local emergency contacts is essential in an emergency. In Japan, dial 119 in case of a fire or medical emergency and 110 for police assistance. Keep your hotel's address and phone number close at hand in case you need to contact the authorities.

Health and Medical Services

a) Health Precautions: Yokohama maintains high health standards, and tap water is safe to drink. It is advisable to carry necessary medications and travel insurance that covers medical emergencies.

Tap water in Yokohama is safe for consumption. However, carrying a reusable water bottle and refilling it from public fountains can reduce plastic waste during your trip. Additionally, have a basic first-aid kit and any required medications with you.

b) Medical Services: Yokohama boasts state-of-the-art hospitals and medical facilities that can manage both urgent situations and standard medical treatment. Some hospitals and clinics offer medical care in the English language.

Visit the closest hospital or clinic for assistance in the event of a medical emergency. To facilitate contact with overseas patients, some medical facilities in Yokohama have English-speaking staff members.

A smooth and pleasurable trip in Yokohama depends on being well-prepared with useful information. Travelers can confidently and respectfully navigate the city by being aware of their alternatives for transportation, money exchange services, cultural etiquette, and emergency contacts. Making the most of your stay in Yokohama while maintaining caution, safety awareness, and preparedness for any medical need will allow you to treasure your experiences and create enduring memories in this dynamic and culturally rich city.

CHAPTER THIRTEEN:
Appendix

30 Useful Phrases in Japanese with Pronunciation Guide

Here are 30 essential phrases in Japanese, along with their pronunciation guide, to help travelers communicate effectively during their visit to Yokohama:

1. Hello - こんにちは (Konnichiwa) - kohn-nee-chee-wah
2. Goodbye - さようなら (Sayounara) - sah-yoh-nah-rah
3. Thank you - ありがとう (Arigatou) - ah-ree-gah-toh
4. Yes - はい (Hai) - hah-ee
5. No - いいえ (Iie) - ee-eh

6. Excuse me - すみません (Sumimasen) - soo-mee-mah-sen

7. Please - お願いします (Onegaishimasu) - oh-neh-gah-ee-shee-mahs

8. Sorry - ごめんなさい (Gomen nasai) - goh-men-nah-sigh

9. I don't understand - わかりません (Wakarimasen) - wah-kah-ree-mah-sen

10. Yes, I understand - はい、わかります (Hai, wakarimasu) - hah-ee, wah-kah-ree-mahs

11. How much is this? - これはいくらですか？ (Kore wa ikura desu ka?) - koh-reh wah ee-koo-rah deh-soo kah?

12. Where is the restroom? - トイレはどこですか？(Toire wa doko desu ka?) - toy-reh wah doh-koh deh-soo kah?

13. Help! - 助けて！(Tasukete!) - tah-soo-keh-teh

14. I need a doctor - 医者が必要です (Isha ga hitsuyou desu) - ee-shah gah hee-tsoo-yoh deh-soo

15. I'm lost - 道に迷いました (Michi ni mayoimashita) - mee-chee nee mah-yoh-ee-mah-shee-tah

16. What time is it? - 今何時ですか？(Ima nanji desu ka?) - ee-mah nah-n-jee deh-soo kah?

17. Can you speak English? - 英語を話せますか？(Eigo o hanasemasu ka?) - ay-goh oh hah-nah-seh-mahs kah?

18. I want... - ...が欲しいです (... ga hoshii desu) - ... gah hoh-shee deh-soo

19. Where is the nearest train station? - 最寄りの駅はどこですか？(Moyori no eki wa doko desu ka?) - moh-yoh-ree noh eh-kee wah doh-koh deh-soo kah?

20. Can you help me find this address? - この住所を探すのを手伝ってくれますか？(Kono

juusho o sagasu no o tetsudatte kuremasu ka?) - koh-noh joo-shoh oh sah-gah-soo noh oh teh-tsoo-daht-teh koo-reh-mahs kah?

21. What is your name? - お名前は何ですか？ (Onamae wa nan desu ka?) - oh-nah-mah-eh wah nahn deh-soo kah?

22. My name is... - 私の名前は...です (Watashi no namae wa... desu) - wah-tah-shee noh nah-mah-eh wah... deh-soo

23. Cheers! (when toasting) - 乾杯！ (Kanpai!) - kahn-pie

24. I love Yokohama! - 横浜が大好きです！ (Yokohama ga daisuki desu!) - yoh-koh-hah-mah gah dah-ee-skhee deh-soo

25. Could you take a photo, please? - 写真を撮っていただけますか？(Shashin o totte itadakemasu ka?) - shah-shin oh toh-teh ee-tah-dah-keh-mahs kah?

26. Is this seat taken? - この席は空いています
か？(Kono seki wa aiteimasu ka?) - koh-noh
se-kee wah ah-ee-teh-ee-mahs kah?

27. How do I get to...? - ...に行くにはどうすれば
いいですか？(... ni iku ni wa dou sureba ii desu
ka?) - ... nee ee-koo nee wah doh soo-reh-bah ee
deh-soo kah?

28. Where can I find a good restaurant? - おいし
いレストランはどこにありますか？(Oishii
resutoran wa doko ni arimasu ka?) - oh-ee-shee
res-toh-rahn wah doh-koh nee ah-ree-mahs kah?

29. Can I pay by card? - カードで払うことができ
ますか？(Kaado de harau koto ga dekimasu
ka?) - kah-doh deh hah-rah-oo koh-toh gah
deh-kee-mahs kah?

30. Do you have any recommendations? - 何か
おすすめはありますか？(Nanika osusume wa
arimasu ka?) - nah-nee-kah oh-soo-soo-meh wah
ah-ree-mahs kah?

Currency Conversion Chart

- 1 USD (US Dollar) ≈ 110 JPY (Japanese Yen)

- 1 EUR (Euro) ≈ 130 JPY

- 1 GBP (British Pound Sterling) ≈ 150 JPY

- 1 AUD (Australian Dollar) ≈ 80 JPY

- 1 CAD (Canadian Dollar) ≈ 90 JPY

- 1 CNY (Chinese Yuan) ≈ 16 JPY

- 1 KRW (South Korean Won) ≈ 0.09 JPY

- 1 INR (Indian Rupee) ≈ 1.5 JPY

- 1 SGD (Singapore Dollar) ≈ 80 JPY

- 1 MYR (Malaysian Ringgit) ≈ 25 JPY

Please note that these rates are based on historical data and are subject to fluctuations in the foreign exchange market. Currency exchange rates can change frequently, so it's essential to check with a reliable source for the most up-to-date rates before making any financial transactions or travel plans involving currency conversion. Banks, currency exchange offices, and financial websites are reliable places to get the latest currency exchange information.

Packing List for Yokohama

A well-prepared packing list can ensure a comfortable and enjoyable trip to Yokohama. Consider the following items to pack for your journey:

Clothing:

- Weather-appropriate clothing: Lightweight and breathable fabrics for summer, and warm layers for winter.

- Comfortable walking shoes: Yokohama is a city best explored on foot, so comfortable shoes are essential.

- Raincoat or umbrella: For unpredictable weather, especially during the rainy season.

- Swimwear: If visiting during the summer months to enjoy the beaches.

Travel Essentials:

- Passport and travel documents: Including visa (if required), flight tickets, and hotel reservations.

- Travel adapters and chargers: Japan uses Type A and Type B electrical outlets (100V).

- Portable charger: To keep your devices charged on the go.

- Personal toiletries: Bring your preferred toiletries as you may not find your preferred brands in Japan.

Health and Safety:

- Prescription medications: Bring enough medication for your entire trip and carry prescriptions.

- First-aid kit: Including adhesive bandages, pain relievers, antiseptic wipes, etc.

- Sunscreen and sunglasses: To protect yourself from the sun's rays.

- Insect repellent: Especially during the summer months.

Electronics:

- Camera or smartphone: For capturing memories of your trip.

- Portable Wi-Fi device: If your accommodation does not provide Wi-Fi, consider renting a portable device for internet access on the go.

Miscellaneous:

- Reusable water bottle: To stay hydrated and reduce plastic waste.

- Travel guidebook or map: For easy navigation and information on local attractions.

- Japanese phrasebook: To aid in communication with locals.

- Foldable bag or backpack: Useful for carrying souvenirs or groceries.

Hand-Picked Hotel Recommendations for Every Budget

Yokohama offers a wide range of accommodation options, catering to different budgets and preferences. Here are some hand-picked hotel recommendations for every budget:

Budget Options:

1. Sakuragicho Washington Hotel: A budget-friendly hotel located near Yokohama's major attractions and public transportation. The hotel offers clean and comfortable rooms with essential amenities.

2. Hostel Zen Yokohama: Ideal for budget travelers, this hostel provides dormitory-style accommodation with communal spaces and a friendly atmosphere.

3. APA Hotel Yokohama Kannai: A value-for-money hotel in the Kannai area, offering compact rooms with modern amenities and easy access to local sights.

Mid-Range Options:

1. Yokohama Bay Sheraton Hotel & Towers: Located in Minato Mirai, this hotel offers comfortable rooms with beautiful bay views and excellent facilities, including a fitness center and restaurants.

2. Hotel New Grand: A historic hotel with a mix of modern and classic charm, offering well-appointed rooms and a range of dining options.

3. Yokohama Royal Park Hotel: Situated in the Landmark Tower, this hotel provides luxurious rooms, stunning city views, and top-notch amenities.

Luxury Options:

1. The Yokohama Bay Hotel Tokyu: A luxurious hotel with stylish rooms overlooking the bay, featuring fine dining options and an elegant ambiance.

2. InterContinental Yokohama Grand: Offering spacious rooms and suites with panoramic bay views, this hotel boasts a spa, multiple restaurants, and top-notch service.

3. Hotel New Otani Yokohama: A luxury hotel featuring opulent rooms, beautiful gardens, and a selection of high-class restaurants and bars.

The appendix section serves as a handy resource for travelers visiting Yokohama. With 30 useful phrases in Japanese, a currency conversion chart, a packing list, and hand-picked hotel recommendations for every budget, travelers can navigate the city confidently, communicate effectively with locals, make informed financial decisions, pack appropriately for their journey, and choose the perfect accommodation to suit their preferences and budget. Armed with this practical information, travelers can embark on a memorable and enjoyable trip to Yokohama, embracing its vibrant culture, rich history, and diverse offerings with ease and confidence.

MAP OF YOKOHAMA

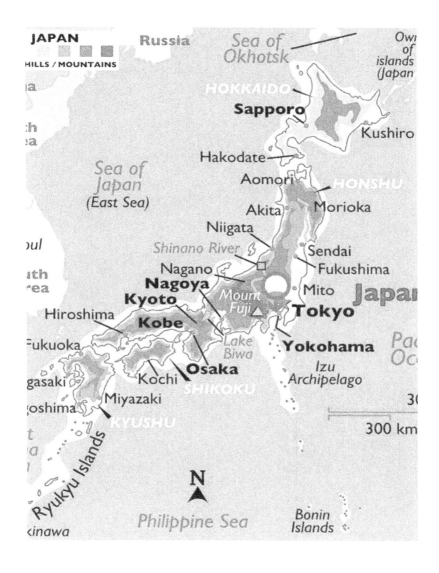